SNOWY DAY
Stories and Poems

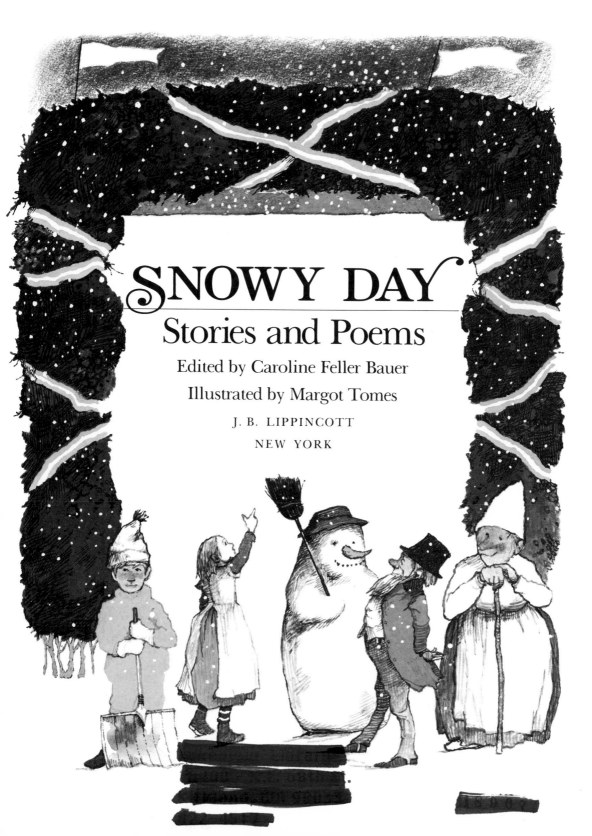

SNOWY DAY

Stories and Poems

Edited by Caroline Feller Bauer

Illustrated by Margot Tomes

J. B. LIPPINCOTT

NEW YORK

FOR BEV BRAUN

who knows that when it snows—you read a book

Snowy Day: Stories and Poems
Text copyright © 1986 by Caroline Feller Bauer
Illustrations copyright © 1986 by Margot Tomes
All rights reserved. No part of this book may be
used or reproduced in any manner whatsoever without
written permission except in the case of brief quotations
embodied in critical articles and reviews. Printed in
the United States of America. For information address
J.B. Lippincott Junior Books, 10 East 53rd Street,
New York, N.Y. 10022. Published simultaneously in
Canada by Fitzhenry & Whiteside Limited, Toronto.

Library of Congress Cataloging-in-Publication Data
Snowy day.

Summary: A collection of stories and poems with
snow as a common theme.
1. Snow—Literary collections. [1. Snow—Literary
collections] I. Bauer, Caroline Feller. II. Tomes,
Margot, ill.
PZ5.S67 1986   808.8′36   85-45858
ISBN 0-397-32176-7
ISBN 0-397-32177-5 (lib. bdg.)

Designed by Constance Fogler
2 3 4 5 6 7 8 9 10

ACKNOWLEDGMENTS

Every effort has been made to trace ownership of all copyright material and to secure the necessary permissions to reprint these selections. In the event of any question arising as to the use of any material, the editor and the publisher, while expressing regret for any inadvertent error, will be happy to make the necessary correction in future printings. Thanks are due to the following for permission to reprint the copyrighted materials listed below:

Addison-Wesley Publishing Company, for "Snow Woman" from *Blueberries Lavender* by Nancy Dingman Watson. Copyright © 1977 Addison Wesley, Reading, Massachusetts. Reprinted with permission. / N. M. Bodecker, for "Footprints of a Sparrow" from *Snowman Sniffles*. Copyright © 1983 by N. M. Bodecker (A Margaret K. McElderry Book). Reprinted with the permission of Atheneum Publishers, Inc. / Charlotte B. DeForest, for "A Lost Snowflake" from *Prancing Pony* by Charlotte B. DeForest, published by Walker/Weatherhill, 1968. / Aileen Fisher, for "Snowball Wind" from *In the Woods, In the Meadow, In the Sky*, Scribner, N.Y., 1965. By permission of the author. / Harcourt Brace Jovanovich, Inc., for "And Then" by Prince Redcloud, from *Moments: Poems for All Seasons*, copyright © 1980 by Lee Bennett Hopkins. Reprinted by permission of Harcourt Brace Jovanovich, Inc. / Harper & Row, Publishers, Inc., for "Cynthia in the Snow" from *Bronzville Boys and Girls* by Gwendolyn Brooks. Copyright © 1956 by Gwendolyn Brooks Blakely; "First Snow" from *A Pocketful of Poems* by Marie Louise Allen. Copyright © 1939 by Harper & Row, Publishers, Inc.; "First Snowfall" from *Cold Stars and Fireflies* by Barbara Juster Esbensen (Thomas Y. Crowell, Co.). Copyright © 1984 by Barbara Juster Esbensen; "Please Bird" from *Flower Moon Snow: A Book of Haiku* by Kazue Mizumura (Thomas Y. Crowell, Co.). Copyright © 1977 by Kazue Mizumura; "Snow" and "Joe's Snow Clothes" from *Dogs and Dragons, Trees and Dreams* by Karla Kuskin. Copyright © 1980 by Karla Kuskin; "The Snow in Chelm" (pp. 29–34) from *Zlateh the Goat and Other Stories* by Isaac Bashevis Singer. Copyright © 1966 by Isaac Bashevis Singer; "Snowy Benches" from *Out in the Dark and Daylight* by Aileen Fisher. Copyright © 1980 by Aileen Fisher. Reprinted by permission of Harper & Row, Publishers, Inc. / Holiday House, for "Winter" reprinted from *A Circle of Seasons* by permission of Holiday House. Copyright © 1982 by Myra Cohn Livingston. / Houghton Mifflin Company, for "Read This with Gestures" from *Fast and Slow* by John Ciardi. Copyright © by John Ciardi. Reprinted by permission of Houghton Mifflin Company. / Hutchinson Publishing Group Limited, for "Don't go, Jo!" from *Over & Over Again* by Barbara Ireson, Beaver/Hanlyn, 1978. / X. J. Kennedy, "Moonwalk" from *The Forgetful Wishing Well*. Copyright © 1985 by X. J. Kennedy (A Margaret K. McElderry Book). Reprinted with the permission of Atheneum Publishers, Inc. / Ray Lincoln Literary Agency, for "December Leaves" from *Don't Ever Cross A Crocodile* by Kaye Starbird. Copyright © 1963 by Kaye Starbird; "The Snowstorm" from *The Pheasant on Route Seven* by Kaye Starbird. Copyright © 1968 by Kaye Starbird. Reprinted by permission of Ray Lincoln Literary Agency. / Little, Brown and Company, for "Joe" from *One at a Time* by David McCord. Copyright © 1952 by Joe McCord; "Winter Morning" from *Custard and Company* by Ogden Nash. Copyright © 1961 by Ogden Nash. By permission of Little, Brown and Company. / Macmillan of Canada, for "Lying on Things" from *Alligator Pie* by Dennis Lee. Reprinted by permission of Macmillan of Canada, A Division of Canada Publishing Company. / Lilian Moore, for "Snowy Morning" from *I Thought I Heard the City*. Text copyright © 1969 Lilian Moore. Reprinted with the permission of Atheneum Publishers, Inc. / William Morrow & Company, for "The Cheerful Snowman" from *Hello, Small Sparrow* by Hannah Lyons Johnson (Lothrop, Lee & Shepard Books, 1971); "It Fell in the City..." from *Blackberry Ink* by Eve Merriam. Copyright © 1985 by Eve Merriam, by permission of William Morrow & Company. / Yoshiko Uchida, for "New Year's Hats for the Statues" from *The Sea of Gold* by Yoshiko Uchida. Copyright © 1965 by Yoshiko Uchida. Reprinted by permission of the author. / The University of Georgia Press, for "Snowflake Soufflé" from *Cross Ties* by X. J. Kennedy, copyright © 1985 by X. J. Kennedy, published by the University of Georgia Press. / Viking Penguin, Inc., for "Snow" from *Yellow Butter Purple Jelly Red Jam Black Bread* by Mary Ann Hoberman. Copyright © 1981 by Mary Ann Hoberman. Reprinted by permission of Viking Penguin, Inc. / Walker & Co., for "A Lost Snowflake" from *Prancing Pony* by Charlotte B. DeForest. Copyright © 1968. Reprinted with permission by Walker & Co. / The Westminster Press, for "Winter Is Tacked Down" from *It's Winter* by Sister Noemi Weygant, O.S.B. Copyright © MCMLXIX Sister Neomi Weygant, O.S.B., used by permission of the Westminster Press. / Suk-Joong Yoon, for "Snowflakes" from *Half Past Four* by Suk-Joong Yoon, published by F. T. Yoon Co., 1978.

Contents

New Year's Hats for the Statues, A Story
Yoshiko Uchida   3

Winter Is Tacked Down   *Sister Noemi Weygant*   12

Snow   *Mary Ann Hoberman*   14

Snowy Benches   *Aileen Fisher*   15

Cynthia in the Snow   *Gwendolyn Brooks*   16

A Lost Snowflake   *Charlotte B. DeForest*   17

It Fell in the City   *Eve Merriam*   18

Winter Morning   *Ogden Nash*   20

Snowflake Soufflé   *X. J. Kennedy*   21

Snowy Day Recipes   22

The Snow in Chelm, A Story
Isaac Bashevis Singer   25

That Cheerful Snowman   *Hannah Lyons Johnson*   30

Footprints of a Sparrow   *N. M. Bodecker*   31

vii

Snow Woman   *Nancy Dingman Watson*   32

Joe   *David McCord*   34

Please Bird   *Kazue Mizumura*   35

First Snowfall   *Barbara Juster Esbensen*   36

Snowy Morning   *Lilian Moore*   37

Snowball Wind   *Aileen Fisher*   38

And Then   *Prince Redcloud*   39

Lying on Things   *Dennis Lee*   40

Snow   *Karla Kuskin*   41

Snowy Day Facts and Activities   42

Marika the Snowmaiden, A Story
   retold by Caroline Feller Bauer   45

The Snowstorm   *Kaye Starbird*   50

Read This with Gestures   *John Ciardi*   51

First Snow   *Marie Louise Allen*   52

Winter   *Myra Cohn Livingston*   53

Joe's Snow Clothes   *Karla Kuskin*   54

December Leaves   *Kaye Starbird*   56

Snowflakes *Suk-Joong Yoon*   57

Moonwalk *X. J. Kennedy*   58

Don't go, Jo! *Barbara Ireson*   59

Snowy Day Activities   60

READ ABOUT SNOW   63

INDEX   67

Snow. Snow is beautiful. It floats down to earth and makes everything look fresh and new and clean. Snow. Skiers love it. Watch them as they glide down the slope. Snow. Children love it. See them making snow angels on the lawn. And snowmen certainly love snow!

Authors and poets think about snow. They write about it too. They write about the snow that falls on the city, covering park benches and sidewalks and streets. They write about snowflakes and snowballs and snowy, snowy days.

So, put on your parka. Pull on your boots and
READ ABOUT SNOW.

SNOWY DAY
Stories and Poems

New Year's Hats for the Statues

YOSHIKO UCHIDA

*All over the world there are fairytales and folktales with a
theme of kindness repaid. This story, from Japan, is about a
man who feels sorry for six statues.*

Once a very kind old man and woman lived in a small
house high in the hills of Japan. Although they were good
people, they were very, very poor, for the old man made his
living by weaving the reed hats that farmers wore to ward
off the sun and rain, and even in a year's time, he could not
sell very many.

One cold winter day as the year was drawing to an end,
the old woman said to the old man, "Good husband, it will
soon be New Year's Day, but we have nothing in the house
to eat. How will we welcome the new year without even a
pot of fresh rice?" A worried frown hovered over her face,

and she sighed sadly as she looked into her empty cupboards.

But the old man patted her shoulders and said, "Now, now, don't you worry. I will make some reed hats and take them to the village to sell. Then with the money I earn I will buy some fish and rice for our New Year's feast."

On the day before New Year's, the old man set out for the village with five new reed hats that he had made. It was bitterly cold, and from early morning, snow tumbled from the skies and blew in great drifts about their small house. The old man shivered in the wind, but he thought about the fresh warm rice and the fish turning crisp and brown over the charcoal, and he knew he must earn some money to buy them. He pulled his wool scarf tighter about his throat and plodded on slowly over the snow-covered roads.

When he got to the village, he trudged up and down its narrow streets calling, "Reed hats for sale! Reed hats for sale!" But everyone was too busy preparing for the new year to be bothered with reed hats. They scurried by him, going instead to the shops where they could buy sea bream and red beans and herring roe for their New Year's feasts. No one even bothered to look at the old man or his hats.

As the old man wandered about the village, the snow

fell faster, and before long the sky began to grow dark. The old man knew it was useless to linger, and he sighed with longing as he passed the fish shop and saw the rows of fresh fish.

"If only I could bring home one small piece of fish for my wife," he thought glumly, but his pockets were even emptier than his stomach.

There was nothing to do but to go home again with his five unsold hats. The old man headed wearily back toward his little house in the hills, bending his head against the biting cold of the wind. As he walked along, he came upon six stone statues of Jizo, the guardian god of children. They stood by the roadside covered with snow that had piled in small drifts on top of their heads and shoulders.

"*Mah, mah,* you are covered with snow," the old man said to the statues, and setting down his bundle, he stopped to brush the snow from their heads. As he was about to go on, a fine idea occurred to him.

"I am sorry these are only reed hats I could not sell," he apologized, "but at least they will keep the snow off your heads." And carefully he tied one on each of the Jizo statues.

"Now if I had one more there would be enough for each of them," he murmured as he looked at the row of statues. But the old man did not hesitate for long. Quickly he took the hat from his own head and tied it on the head of the sixth statue.

"There," he said looking pleased. "Now all of you are covered." Then, bowing in farewell, he told the statues that he must be going. "A happy New Year to each of you," he called, and he hurried away content.

When he got home the old woman was waiting anxiously for him. "Did you sell your hats?" she asked. "Were you able to buy some rice and fish?"

The old man shook his head. "I couldn't sell a single hat," he explained, "but I did find a very good use for them." And he told her how he had put them on the Jizo statues that stood in the snow.

"Ah, that was a very kind thing to do," the old woman said. "I would have done exactly the same." And she did not complain at all that the old man had not brought home anything to eat. Instead she made some hot tea and added a precious piece of charcoal to the brazier so the old man could warm himself.

That night they went to bed early, for there was no more charcoal and the house had grown cold. Outside the wind continued to blow the snow in a white curtain that wrapped itself about the small house. The old man and woman huddled beneath their thick quilts and tried to keep warm.

"We are fortunate to have a roof over our heads on such a night," the old man said.

"Indeed we are," the old woman agreed, and before long they were both fast asleep.

About daybreak, when the sky was still a misty gray, the old man awakened for he heard voices outside.

"Listen," he whispered to the old woman.

"What is it? What is it?" the old woman asked.

Together they held their breath and listened. It sounded like a group of men pulling a very heavy load.

"*Yoi-sah! Hoi-sah! Yoi-sah! Hoi-sah!*" the voices called and seemed to come closer and closer.

"Who could it be so early in the morning?" the old man wondered. Soon, they heard the men singing:

Where is the home of the kind old man,
The man who covered our heads?
Where is the home of the kind old man,
Who gave us his hats for our heads?

The old man and woman hurried to the window to look out, and there in the snow they saw the six stone Jizo statues lumbering toward their house. They still wore the reed hats the old man had given them and each one was pulling a heavy sack.

"*Yoi-sah! Hoi-sah! Yoi-sah! Hoi-sah!*" they called as they drew nearer and nearer.

"They seem to be coming here!" the old man gasped in amazement. But the old woman was too surprised even to speak.

As they watched, each of the Jizo statues came up to their house and left his sack at the doorstep.

The old man hurried to open the door, and as he did, the six big sacks came tumbling inside. In the sacks the old man and woman found rice and wheat, fish and beans, wine and bean paste cakes, and all sorts of delicious things that they might want to eat.

"Why, there is enough here for a feast every day all during the year!" the old man cried excitedly.

"And we shall have the finest New Year's feast we have ever had in our lives," the old woman exclaimed.

"Ojizo Sama, thank you!" the old man shouted.

"Ojizo Sama, how can we thank you enough?" the old woman called out.

10

But the six stone statues were already moving slowly down the road, and as the old man and woman watched, they disappeared into the whiteness of the falling snow, leaving only their footprints to show that they had been there at all.

Winter Is Tacked Down

SISTER NOEMI WEYGANT

Hurrah!

Hurray!

It snowed last night.

Today
    the green lawn
    is whiskered with white.

Look around—
    enough snow on the ground
    for a snowball.

Scoop it up in your hands,
    gloves or no.
Wad it,
    pack it tight,
      round,
      big.

Let go!

Smash!
Splash!

Winter is here!

You can't hold winter back,
    not possibly,
        once you have tacked a snowball
        to the trunk of a tree.

Snow

MARY ANN HOBERMAN

Snow
Snow
Lots of snow
Everywhere we look and everywhere we go
Snow in the sandbox
Snow on the slide
Snow on the bicycle
Left outside
Snow on the steps
And snow on my feet
Snow on the sidewalk
Snow on the sidewalk
Snow on the sidewalk
Down the street.

Snowy Benches

AILEEN FISHER

Do parks get lonely
in winter, perhaps,
when benches have only
snow on their laps?

Cynthia in the Snow

GWENDOLYN BROOKS

IT SUSHES.
It hushes
The loudness in the road.
It flitter-twitters,
And laughs away from me.
It laughs a lovely whiteness,
And whitely whirs away,
To be
Some otherwhere,
Still white as milk or shirts.
So beautiful it hurts.

A Lost Snowflake

CHARLOTTE B. DEFOREST

The snowflakes fell, the first this year.
I caught one on my sleeve—right here!
I thought that we would play all day.
But then it melted—right away!

It Fell in the City

EVE MERRIAM

It fell in the city,
It fell through the night,
And the black rooftops
All turned white.

Red fire hydrants
All turned white.
Blue police cars
All turned white.

Green garbage cans
All turned white.
Gray sidewalks
All turned white.

Yellow No PARKING signs
All turned white
When it fell in the city
All through the night.

Winter Morning

OGDEN NASH

Winter is the king of showmen,
Turning tree stumps into snow men
And houses into birthday cakes
And spreading sugar over the lakes.
Smooth and clean and frost white
The world looks good enough to bite.
That's the season to be young,
Catching snowflakes on your tongue.

Snow is snowy when it's snowing
I'm sorry it's slushy when it's going.

Snowflake Soufflé

X. J. KENNEDY

Snowflake soufflé
Snowflake soufflé
Makes a lip-smacking lunch
On an ice-cold day!

You take seven snowflakes,
You break seven eggs,
And you stir it seven times
With your two hind legs.

Bake it in an igloo,
Throw it on a plate,
And slice off a slice
With a rusty ice-skate.

Snow Muffins from Northern Canada

You need:

- 2 cups sifted flour
- 3 teaspoons baking powder
- ½ cup sugar
- ½ teaspoon salt
- ¾ cup milk
- 3 tablespoons melted butter
- ½ teaspoon grated orange rind or lemon rind
- ½ cup clean snow
- ½ cup raisins

To make:

Sift flour, baking powder, sugar and salt into a bowl. Make a well in the center of the dry ingredients. Add milk, melted butter and grated rind. Stir lightly with a fork.

Add snow and raisins and mix lightly. Spoon batter into 12 greased muffin tins. Bake at 400° for 15–18 minutes.

Snow Pudding *or* Oeufs a la Neige

You need:

> One package soft vanilla custard
>
> 3 egg whites
>
> 6 tablespoons sugar and a pinch of salt

To make:

> Prepare pudding according to package directions and let set in a large bowl.
>
> Beat egg whites until very stiff. Add salt and sugar gradually. Drop by tablespoons into boiling water. When meringue is set, remove from water with a slotted spoon and place on pudding.

The Snow in Chelm

ISAAC BASHEVIS SINGER

*It's snowing. Look outside. Isn't the snow beautiful, sparkling
in the moonlight? What does it look like? Silver? Pearls?
Diamonds? The seven foolish elders of Chelm wanted to
harvest this wonderful treasure that falls from the sky.*

Chelm was a village of fools, fools young and old. One
night someone spied the moon reflected in a barrel of water.
The people of Chelm imagined it had fallen in. They sealed
the barrel so that the moon would not escape. When the
barrel was opened in the morning and the moon wasn't
there, the villagers decided it had been stolen. They sent for
the police, and when the thief couldn't be found, the fools
of Chelm cried and moaned.

Of all the fools of Chelm, the most famous were its
seven Elders. Because they were the village's oldest and
greatest fools, they ruled in Chelm. They had white beards
and high foreheads from too much thinking.

Once, on a Hanukkah night, the snow fell all evening.
It covered all of Chelm like a silver tablecloth. The moon

25

shone; the stars twinkled; the snow shimmered like pearls and diamonds.

That evening the seven Elders were sitting and pondering, wrinkling their foreheads. The village was in need of money, and they did not know where to get it. Suddenly the oldest of them all, Gronam the Great Fool, exclaimed, "The snow is silver!"

"I see pearls in the snow!" another shouted.

"And I see diamonds!" a third called out.

It became clear to the Elders of Chelm that a treasure had fallen from the sky.

But soon they began to worry. The people of Chelm liked to go walking, and they would most certainly trample the treasure. What was to be done? Silly Tudras had an idea.

"Let's send a messenger to knock on all the windows and let the people know that they must remain in their houses until all the silver, all the pearls, and all the diamonds are safely gathered up."

For a while the Elders were satisfied. They rubbed their hands in approval of the clever idea. But then Dopey Lekisch called out in consternation, "The messenger himself will trample the treasure."

The Elders realized that Lekisch was right, and again

they wrinkled their high foreheads in an effort to solve the problem.

"I've got it!" exclaimed Shmerel the Ox.

"Tell us, tell us," pleaded the Elders.

"The messenger must not go on foot. He must be carried on a table so that his feet will not tread on the precious snow."

Everybody was delighted with Shmerel the Ox's solution; and the Elders, clapping their hands, admired their own wisdom.

The Elders immediately sent to the kitchen for Gimpel the errand boy and stood him on a table. Now who was going to carry the table? It was lucky that in the kitchen there were Treitle the cook, Berel the potato peeler, Yukel the salad mixer, and Yontel, who was in charge of the community goat. All four were ordered to lift up the table on which Gimpel stood. Each one took hold of a leg. On top stood Gimpel, grasping a wooden hammer with which to tap on the villagers' windows. Off they went.

At each window Gimpel knocked with the hammer and called out, "No one leaves the house tonight. A treasure has fallen from the sky, and it is forbidden to step on it."

The people of Chelm obeyed the Elders and remained

in their houses all night. Meanwhile the Elders themselves sat up trying to figure out how to make the best use of the treasure once it had been gathered up.

Silly Tudras proposed that they sell it and buy a goose which lays golden eggs. Thus the community would be provided with a steady income.

Dopey Lekisch had another idea. Why not buy eye-glasses that make things look bigger for all the inhabitants of Chelm? Then the houses, the streets, the stores would all look bigger, and of course if Chelm *looked* bigger, then it *would be* bigger. It would no longer be a village, but a big city.

There were other, equally clever ideas. But while the Elders were weighing their various plans, morning came and the sun rose. They looked out of the window, and, alas, they saw the snow had been trampled. The heavy boots of the table carriers had destroyed the treasure.

The Elders of Chelm clutched at their white beards and admitted to one another that they had made a mistake. Perhaps, they reasoned, four others should have carried the four men who had carried the table that held Gimpel the errand boy?

After long deliberations the Elders decided that if next Hanukkah a treasure would again fall down from the sky, that is exactly what they would do.

Although the villagers remained without a treasure, they were full of hope for the next year and praised their Elders, who they knew could always be counted on to find a way, no matter how difficult the problem.

29

That Cheerful Snowman

HANNAH LYONS JOHNSON

That cheerful snowman
Guarding our door
Never will
See our daffodils.

Footprints of a Sparrow

N. M. BODECKER

Footprints of a sparrow
in the new, clean snow.

And there, now, right on top of them,
the scratchings of a crow!

Clearly, and without a doubt,
what the sparrow wrote about
angrily the crow scratched out...

would you not like to know
what sort of sparrow silliness
did aggravate that crow?

Snow Woman

NANCY DINGMAN WATSON

Snow woman snow woman
What do you know?
You sit so still
And silent in the snow.

Snow woman snow woman
Do you like your hat?
You sit so quiet
And comfortable and fat.

Snow woman snow woman
Do you like your clothes?
Your apron and your mittens
And your big carrot nose?

Snow woman snow woman
Sitting in the night
Does the dark scare you
Or the cold moonlight?

Snow woman snow woman
Here comes the sun
Are you afraid of melting
And being all done?

Joe

DAVID MCCORD

We feed the birds in winter,
And outside in the snow
We have a tray of many seeds
For many birds of many breeds
And one gray squirrel named Joe.
    But Joe comes early,
    Joe comes late,
    And all the birds
    Must stand and wait.
And waiting there for Joe to go
Is pretty cold work in the snow.

Please Bird

KAZUE MIZUMURA

Please bird, don't go yet.
You are the finishing touch
To the snowy branch.

First Snowfall

BARBARA JUSTER ESBENSEN

Out of the grey
pinched air
it falls.

We hear it in the oak trees
hissing
through the brown tongues
of leaves
whispering
and sifting down.

Soon it will erase
the way to school
and our feet will blunder
in blind boots.

Lashes will be fringed
with snowflakes
and our tongues will taste
the cold vanilla
of this early winter day.

Snowy Morning

LILIAN MOORE

Wake
gently this morning
to a different day.
Listen.

There is no bray
of buses,
no brake growls,
no siren howls and
no horns
blow.

There is only
the silence
of a city
hushed
by snow.

Snowball Wind

AILEEN FISHER

The wind was throwing snowballs.
It plucked them from the trees
and tossed them all around the woods
as boldly as you please.

I ducked beneath the spruces
which didn't help a speck;
the wind kept throwing snowballs
and threw one down my neck.

And Then

PRINCE REDCLOUD

I was reading
a poem
about snow

when
the sun
came out
and
melted it.

Lying on Things

DENNIS LEE

After it snows
I go and lie on things.

I lie on my back
And make snow-angel wings.

I lie on my front
And powder-puff my nose.

I *always* lie on things
Right after it snows.

Snow

KARLA KUSKIN

We'll play in the snow
And stray in the snow
And stay in the snow
In a snow-white park.
We'll clown in the snow
And frown in the snow
Fall down in the snow
Till it's after dark.
We'll cook snow pies
In a big snow pan.
We'll make snow eyes
In a round snow man.
We'll sing snow songs
And chant snow chants
And roll in the snow
In our fat snow pants.
And when it's time to go home to eat
We'll have snow toes
On our frosted feet.

Snow falls on only a third of the earth's surface, so most people have not seen snow.

Snow looks white because of the reflection of light on the snow crystals. In Greenland microscopic plants sometimes make the snow look red or green.

In Alaska, Eskimo boys and girls play a variant of soccer on a field of snow.

Skis were originally used for transportation. In Hoting, Sweden, skis have been found that may have been made 4500 years ago.

Snowshoes help you walk *on* the snow without sinking *into* the snow. Fat round snowshoes work well where there are no trees. Long skinny snowshoes work best where it is heavily forested.

Snow crystals always have six sides, but they are never exactly the same.

Measuring snow

To make a snow gauge: When a snowstorm is forecast, stand a widemouthed empty can away from trees or buildings. After the snow is collected, let it melt and measure the depth of the water in the can. That measurement will be about one tenth as deep as the snowfall.

In January 1967 snow fell continuously for 29 hours and 8 minutes in the city of Chicago. The city estimated that 24 million tons of snow fell.

Who says you can't change the weather? Scientists have been making artificial snow for ski resorts since 1946.

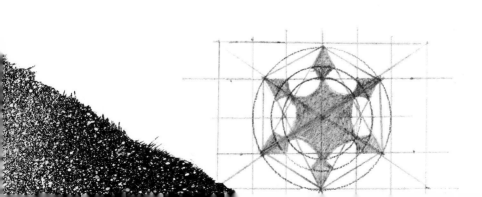

Marika the Snowmaiden

RETOLD BY CAROLINE FELLER BAUER

*This story comes from Russia. It's about a snowmaiden and
something magical that happened one winter day long ago.*

In a mountain town in Russia an old man and woman
lived on a small farm. They had no children and during the
long cold winters they were lonely.

The snows piled up in drifts outside the cottage. The
days passed slowly. The man fed the animals in the small
shed in back of the house. The woman cooked hearty stews.
They had long ago told each other the stories that they
knew, and they longed for a child.

During the cold winter days the old woman sat
huddled by the stove mending their clothes. The old man
repaired the harness for their horse. One day they woke up
to a bright new snowfall.

"Let's go outside and build something in the snow,"
said the old man. The woman thought that a lovely idea
and bundled up in her shawls and muffler and went outside
with her husband. There they rolled a large ball of snow for

the base of the snowmaiden's body and put a smaller ball on top of that one to create a torso and finally a still smaller ball for the head. The old man took a stick and fashioned features into the snow statue's face.

The old woman was delighted. She and her husband stepped back to admire their work. Suddenly something strange began to happen.

It didn't happen all at once. As the couple stood staring at their snow creation, her arms and legs began to emerge from the unsculptured snow. Her body started to take on more form. The features of her face seemed to become clearer. Their snowmaiden was turning into a real live girl.

The old couple soon thought of her as their own daughter. It seemed as though she grew by the hour. After only a few days she had become a lovely young lady. She had the palest of complexions, almost transparent. Her hair was the lightest color of gold and swirled about her face. The old woman called her Marika, and together they spent their days working about the house. Marika was such fun to have around. Her joyous laughter filled the small cottage. Outside in the cold winter snow she helped her father with the animals. After the daily chores were done Marika and her parents would enjoy a walk through the

snow-laden trees in the woods. Marika seemed to enjoy the freezing temperatures and delighted in a good heavy snowfall. In the early morning she would dance through the swirling snowflakes, smiling and laughing.

Then one day winter announced its end. The winds died down and the snow began slowly to melt.

Marika began to act strangely. She didn't laugh as much and began to sit quietly, staring out of the window. Her parents began to worry. Instead of being overjoyed by the appearance of the first spring buds peering through the last of the snow piles, Marika retreated to the shade of the forest and spent the day sitting on the last patch of a snowdrift.

When her parents tried to find out what the problem was, Marika became more and more quiet. The day a warm breeze started to melt the last of the snow on the shadowed side of the house Marika seemed even sadder than before.

Girls and boys from nearby cottages called for Marika to come and play, but she refused. Instead she fashioned a chair from the last of the snow and sat in it, watching her parents at work.

As the first birds began to return singing to the countryside, Marika spent more and more time alone. At last her mother insisted that she join the boys and girls for the first picnic of spring. Marika declined to join in their games of hide and seek. She seemed listless and ill.

"Come play," they called as they began a game of jump the fire. A small fire was set in a clearing and the boys and girls jumped over it in a laughing welcome to spring.

The children stared in horrible fascination. Marika jumped over the flame, and as the heat of the fire rose to meet her, she melted just as a ball of snow might if tossed into a fire.

With a hiss, all that was left of Marika was a small pool of water. The snowmaiden had melted completely away.

The Snowstorm

KAYE STARBIRD

Ever since Tuesday the snow has been falling
And falling and falling
And falling.
No people are stirring, no car-motors whirring,
No chickadees calling.

The bushes are clouds, and the cars sit like igloos
Deserted on roadsides and slopes.
There's wool on the pines, and the telegraph lines
Are sagging white ropes.

With everything changing its shape and its color
On sidewalk and highway and lawn
Or else disappearing from sight or from hearing
As Friday comes on. . . .

It's easy to dream that the snow will keep snowing
And snowing and snowing
And snowing
For week after week, till there's only the peak
Of the church steeple showing.

Read This with Gestures

JOHN CIARDI

It isn't proper, I guess you know,
   To dip your hands—like this—in the snow,
And make a snowball, and look for a hat,
   And try to knock it off—like that!

First Snow

MARIE LOUISE ALLEN

Snow makes whiteness where it falls.
The bushes look like popcorn-balls.
And places where I always play,
Look like somewhere else today.

Winter

MYRA COHN LIVINGSTON

Winter etches windowpanes, fingerpaints in white,
Sculptures strange soft shapes of snow that glister in the
     night,
Filigrees the snowflake, spins icicles of glass,
Paints the ground in hoarfrost, its needles sharp with
     light.

Joe's Snow Clothes

KARLA KUSKIN

For wandering walks
In the sparkling snow
No one is muffled
More warmly than Joe.
No one is mittened more, .
Coated or hatted,
Booted or sweatered,
Both knitted and tatted,
Buttoned and zippered,
Tied, tucked and belted,
Padded and wadded
And quilted and felted,
Hooked in and hooded,
Tweeded and twilled.
Nothing of Joe's
From his top to his toes
But the tip of his nose
Could be touched
By the snows

Or the wind as it blows,
And grow rather rosy,
The way a nose grows
If it's frozen
Or possibly chilled.

December Leaves

KAYE STARBIRD

The fallen leaves are cornflakes
    That fill the lawn's wide dish,
And night and noon
The wind's a spoon
That stirs them with a swish.

The sky's a silver sifter
A-sifting white and slow,
That gently shakes
On crisp brown flakes
The sugar known as snow.

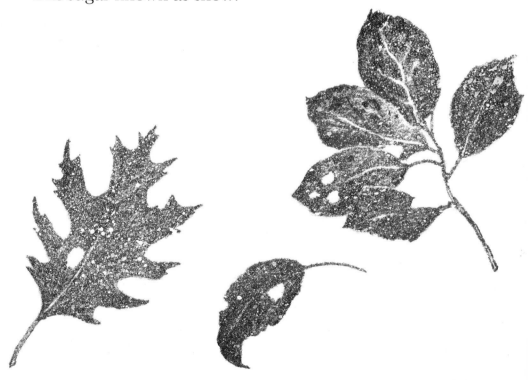

Snowflakes

SUK-JOONG YOON

Snow
Snow
Snow
Let me catch you in my mouth!

Ah
Ah
Ah
The flakes keep landing on my nose!

Ha
Ha
Ha
That's my nose, not my mouth!

Moonwalk

X. J. KENNEDY

Snow kept on sifting through the night,
Now all of earth today
Is one wide moon for me to walk—
Whatever will I weigh?

I want to take a giant step!
Quick, snap my snowsuit snappers!
A moon with not one footprint yet
And no one's candy wrappers!

Don't go, Jo!

BARBARA IRESON

Don't go, don't go, don't go, Jo!
Can't you see the snow, Jo?
If you put your foot outside
It will freeze your toe, Jo!

Make a Marshmallow Snowperson

You need:

    large marshmallows
    miniature marshmallows
    one can vanilla frosting
    raisins
    scissors to cut and shape marshmallows and raisins

To make:

Pretend the marshmallows are balls of snow. The vanilla frosting will hold them together. The raisins are to be used for decoration. They can be used as eyes and mouth or even buttons. Use your imagination to create to snowperson with arms and legs, a head and body.

Noodle Snowflakes

You need:

    several packages of assorted noodles

    white glue

    waxed paper

To make:

    Arrange the noodles in a snowflake design on a
piece of waxed paper. Glue the noodles together and
leave your creation on the waxed paper until it dries.
In about two hours you will be able to peel the
paper away.

    You can hang your noodle snowflake from a
string as a winter decoration.

Read About Snow

PICTURE BOOKS

The Crack-of-Dawn Walkers by Amy Hest. Illustrated by Amy Schwartz. Macmillan. *Sadie and her grandfather take an early morning walk through the snow.*

First Snow by Emily Arnold McCully. Illustrated by the author. Harper & Row. *Enjoy a day in the snow with a family of mice in a wordless picture book.*

Happy Winter by Karen Gundersheimer. Illustrated by the author. Harper & Row. *A little girl tells all about the family fun she has during a snowy winter.*

It Looks Like Snow by Remy Charlip. Illustrated by the author. Greenwillow. *A funny book about Whitey the Eskimo boy and his dog Blanche.*

It's Snowing! It's Snowing! by Jack Prelutsky. Illustrated by Jeanne Titherington. Greenwillow. *Happy, exuberant poems about snow.*

A Prairie Boy's Winter by William Kurelik. Illustrated by the author. Tundra Books. *Winter on the Canadian prairies is shown in text and paintings.*

Snow by Isao Sasaki. Illustrated by the author. Viking. *A wordless picture book shows a train station and the stationmaster in the midst of a snowstorm.*

The Snowman by Raymond Briggs. Illustrated by the author. Random House. *In a wordless picture book a boy builds a snowman and goes on a trip with him.*

The Snowy Day by Ezra Jack Keats. Illustrated by the author. Viking. *A small boy spends a day playing in the snow.*

The Summer Snowman by Margaret Bloy Graham. Illustrated by Gene Zion. Harper & Row. *A little boy saves a tiny snowman in his freezer to enjoy in the summer.*

LONGER BOOKS

The Adventures of Johnny May by Robbie Branscum. Illustrated by Deborah Howland. Harper & Row. *Eleven-year-old Johnny May hunts for a Christmas deer through the snow in the woods.*

Anna, Grandpa, and the Big Storm by Carla Stevens. Clarion. *In the great blizzard of 1888, a little girl and her Grandpa have a memorable adventure.*

Avalanche! by Ron Roy. Dutton. *Scott is buried alive in an avalanche while skiing in Colorado.*

Canyon Winter by Walt Morey. Dutton. *Peter is forced to spend a winter with reclusive Omar in the wilderness areas of the Rockies.*

Day of the Blizzard by Marietta Moskin. Coward McCann. *Katie makes her way through the famous blizzard of 1888 to get a present for Mama.*

A Girl Called Bob and a Horse Called Yoki by Barbara Campbell. Dial. *Two children save a horse from slaughter in the middle of a snowstorm.*

Great Mysteries of the Ice and Snow by Edward F. Dolan, Jr. Dodd, Mead. *Is there really an Abominable Snowman? What happened to the balloonist who tried to fly over the North Pole?*

The Half-a-Moon Inn by Paul Fleischman. Harper & Row. *Mute Aaron wanders through a blizzard to find his mother and finds scheming Miss Grackle and the Half-a-Moon Inn.*

The Hour of the Wolf by Patricia Calvert. Scribners. *Jake enters the Iditarod, a famous dogsled race held in Alaska.*

Ike and Mana and the Once-in-a-Lifetime Movie by Carol Snyder. Coward McCann. *In the midst of a blizzard two friends get a chance to perform in a movie.*

London Snow by Paul Theroux. Houghton. *Two orphans search for their cantankerous landlord in a snowstorm.*

Long Claws: An Arctic Adventure by James Houston. Atheneum. *Pitohok and his sister Upik journey through a storm across the frozen tundra to find food for their family.*

North of Danger by Dale Fife. Dutton. *Arne must ski across a frozen wasteland to warn his father of the Nazi occupation during World War II.*

The Secret Language of Snow by Terry Tempest Williams and Ted Major. Illustrated by Jennifer Dewey. Sierra Club/ Pantheon. *The many types of snow as described by the Inuit people of Alaska are explored in facts and poems.*

Index

Allen, Marie Louise, 52

And Then, 39

Bauer, Caroline Feller, 45

Bodecker, N. M., 31

Brooks, Gwendolyn, 16

Ciardi, John, 51

Cynthia in the Snow, 16

December Leaves, 56

DeForest, Charlotte B., 17

Don't go, Jo!, 59

Esbensen, Barbara Juster, 36

First Snow, 52

First Snowfall, 36

Fisher, Aileen, 15, 38

Footprints of a Sparrow, 31

Hoberman, Mary Ann, 14

Ireson, Barbara, 59

It Fell in the City, 18

Joe, 34

Joe's Snow Clothes, 54

Johnson, Hannah Lyons, 30

Kennedy, X. J., 21, 58

Kuskin, Karla, 41, 54

Lee, Dennis, 40

Livingston, Myra Cohn, 53

A Lost Snowflake, 17

Lying on Things, 40

Marika the Snowmaiden, 45

McCord, David, 34

Merriam, Eve, 18

Mizumura, Kazue, 35

Moonwalk, 58

Moore, Lilian, 37

Nash, Ogden, 20

New Year's Hats for the Statues, 3

Please Bird, 35

Read This with Gestures, 51

Redcloud (Prince), 39

Singer, Isaac Bashevis, 25

Snow, 14

Snow, 41

The Snow in Chelm, 25

Snow Woman, 32

Snowball Wind, 38

Snowflake Soufflé, 21

Snowflakes, 57

The Snowstorm, 50

Snowy Benches, 15

Snowy Morning, 37

Starbird, Kaye, 50, 56

That Cheerful Snowman, 30

Uchida, Yoshiko, 31
Watson, Nancy Dingman, 32
Weygant, Sister Noemi, 12
Winter, 53

Winter Is Tacked Down, 12
Winter Morning, 20
Yoon, Suk-Joong, 57